EX LIBRIS

Workin' in da BONEYARD

Denise Alvarado and
Madrina Angelique

First published in 2012 by Creole Moon Publications

Copyright © 2012 Denise Alvarado and Madrina Angelique

All rights reserved. No part of this publication may be reproduced or transmitted in any form or by any means, electronic, or mechanical, including photocopy, or any information storage and retrieval system, without permission from the authors, except in brief quotations embodied in critical articles and reviews.

ISBN-10: 1480003271 (paper)
EAN-13: 978-1480003279 (paper)

Primary Category: Body, Mind & Spirit/Occultism
Country of Publication: United States
Publication Date: 27th day of the 9th Moon, 2012
Language: English

Library of Congress Cataloging-in-Publication Data pending

Cover design by Denise Alvarado
Cover © Denise Alvarado
Photography © Denise Alvarado
Interior by Denise Alvarado

Typeset in Georgia with Impact, Times New Roman and BN-Old Fashioned

CREOLE MOON
Publications

TABLE OF CONTENTS

Workin' in da Boneyard 1
    Words of Caution 4
Choosing a Cemetery... 8
    Types of Cemeteries 8
    Locating Ancestral Graves..9
Reading Gravestone Signs and Symbols................................... 13
    Animals 14
    Body Parts... 15
    Objects/Other 16
    Trees and Plants.. 18
Gravestone Rubbings... 20
Graveyard Etiquette... 22
    Entering and Leaving 23
The Haunted New Orleans Wishing Tomb 25
    The Campaign to Protect the Tomb of Marie Laveau.......... 28
    The Wishing Ritual 29
Buying Graveyard Dirt.. 31
    Hiring a Spirit 33
Time and Moon Phase Correspondences................................... 38
Grave-type Correspondences.. 42
Graveyard Works 48
    To Make Roommate Move...48
    To Get Rid of Someone... 49
    To Make your Business Grow 49
    To Attract a Lover... 49
    To Keep Someone in Jail 49
    Graveyard Protection Jar 50
    For a Peaceful Home... 50
    Cemetery Money Spell 51
    Gravestone Dust for Good Luck.. 51

To Cut Something from your Life 52
To Stop an Enemy 52
Oya War Water (Santeria) 52
Graveyard Charm for Protection 53
To Break Up a Couple 53
Enemy Jar Spell 53
To Keep Your Boss in Line 54
Beef Tongue Curse 54
Graveyard Gambling Mojo 55
81 Knot Gambling Mojo 55
Graveyard Love Work 56
Oya Offering for Business (Santeria) 56
Stone Bowl 57
To Bring Back a Person 57
To Keep the Law Away 57
Graveyard Rocks to Make Someone Move 58
To Make Someone Leave 58
Bottle Spell to Haunt a Person 58
To Keep the Law Away 59
To Make Someone Return 59
To Get a Job Back 60
To Make a Wish Come True 60
To Make a Person Leave 60
To Make a Person Pine Away 61
To Bury a Bad Habit 61
To Call a Spirit 61
To Make a Person Move Home or Business 62
Cooking Supper for the Dead 62
To Shame Woman To Stop Running Around 63
To Kill Gossip 63
For Good Luck 63
To Cause Confusion Between a Man and His Wife 64

- For Protection Against Enemies 64
- To Cause Conflict 65
- Oya Blessing (Santeria) 65
- Making the Four Corners 65
- To Find Lover 66

FORMULAS 67
- Graveyard Fire Water 67
- Domination Oil 67
- Graveyard Power Dust 68
- Cemetery Oil 68
- Get Away Powder 68
- Confusion Powder 69
- Death Water 69
- Cemetery Nails 69
- Coffin Nail Oil 70

Lagniappe: Goofer Dust 71
- Goofer Dust Formulas 72
- Goofer Dust Work 73
  - Revenge on an Enemy 73
  - To Get a Job 73
  - To Make Person have Sore Feet 73

References 74
Resources 76
About the Authors 78
To Our Readers 80

The wealthiest places in the world are not gold mines, oil fields, diamond mines or banks. The wealthiest place is the cemetery. There lies companies that were never started, masterpieces that were never painted... In the cemetery there is buried the greatest treasure of untapped potential. There is a treasure within you that must come out. Don't go to the grave with your treasure still within YOU. ~ **Dr. Myles Munroe**

WORKING IN DA' BONEYARD

"Every man should keep a fair-sized cemetery in which to bury the faults of his friends."
~ Henry Ward Beecher

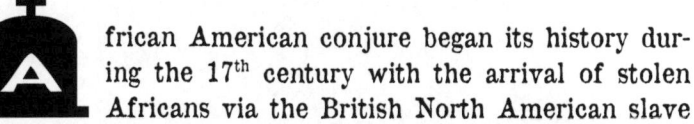

African American conjure began its history during the 17th century with the arrival of stolen Africans via the British North American slave trade. Deposited in the Atlantic coast colonies and New Orleans, slaves from a number of regions in Africa came to influence the development of American Hoodoo in a significant fashion. In the Chesapeake area, the largest population was the Igbo of the Bight of Biafra region of West Africa. In South Carolina and Georgia, there were large populations of slaves from Angola and Kongo. In New Orleans, there was a large population of Senegambians. In each of these regions, there were numerous other African ethnicities that also had their influence on African American conjure. Perhaps the largest cultural influence of all the various slave populations is that of ancestor reverence and the use of graveyard dirt in their charms (Pinn, Finley and Alexander, 2009).

Many slaves imported to the South between 1733 and 1807 were from the Kongo region. Burial customs at the

Grave of Lewis Porter, slave who died 1853 with tombstone erected by his master Major Porter; Fairview Cemetery, Eufaula, Alabama Federal Writer's Project, p.d.

time illustrate the spiritual traditions that were imported with them. For example, graves were decorated with a number of material objects such as shells, dishes, flower pots, letters, jars and personal possessions. To the uninformed, these objects look like simple decorations. Each of these items, however, holds a special cultural meaning in African American cultural history.

Consider the beliefs of the people of lower Zaire, for

example, where the world of the dead is not underground. Instead, it is under water, in the realm of the *bakulu,* the blessed dead. They believed that when a person dies they transform into white creatures that live on river bottoms. Thus, it is the color white that represents death in Central Africa, as opposed to the Western association of death with the color black. This belief is reflected on every grave site where there is a white conch shell.

In fact, conch shells and oyster shells are readily available in the low country of South Carolina and so they are often found on gravesites. Sometimes, they appear to form a sort of barrier or boundary that completely encircles the grave. The barrier of shells and stones appears to delineate the realm of death. Prior to being placed on a grave, however, conch shells are bleached completely white. They are then placed at the foot and head of the grave with smaller shells decorating the border.

More than simply boundaries, shells represent the sea. The sea was the means of transporting slaves to the Americas and it is believed to be the way back home. According to a Gullah woman, Bessie Jones (North by South, n.d.):

The shells stand for the sea. The sea brought us and the sea shall take us back. So the shells upon our graves stand for water, the means of glory and the land of demise.

Some of the offerings found on African American graves hold ancestral memories. According to a number of accounts, coconuts found on graves are believed to have a similar meaning as conch shells. Coconuts have also been a cash crop and a source of food for a very long time in areas in Africa where they grow. It may be that a coconut placed on a grave symbolizes food for the spirit.

Sometimes, burial mounds are found with pipes sticking out of them. This interesting custom reportedly allows communication with the spirit of the grave through a "speaking tube." Leaving letters, photos, and other personal possessions are other ways of communicating with the dead.

Certain bushes and trees are planted in cemeteries to represent the involvement of the living in the life-death-life cycle, as well as to keep memories alive. For example, ivy represents immortality and friendship, while holly protects tombs and graves from lightning strikes.

Among the most common offerings to the deceased are simple candles. Candles are said to represent the souls of the departed. Catholics will often leave candles on graves as a way of showing that prayers have been said for the deceased. Finally, mirrors found in cemeteries are said to "catch the flashing light of the spirit and hold it there" (McMickle, 2002).

Words of Caution

There are some experienced rootworkers who caution against doing graveyard work, and with good reason. It is not something you should rush out to do because it is "scary" or seems "cool". When you walk into a cemetery, you are walking into the realm of the dead, and among the dead are the good, the bad, and the ugly. You are walking among murderers, rapists, child abusers, charlatans and people with every vice imaginable. Just because a person

(Continued on page 6)

GRAVE DECORATIONS

In parts of the Congo "the natives mark the final resting-place of their friends by ornamenting their graves with crockery, empty bottles, old cooking-pots, etc., all of which articles are rendered useless by being cracked or perforated with holes. Were this precaution not taken, the grotesque decoration would be stolen." Broken crockery, along with other articles, is used also in Angola. I have observed this sort of decoration all through the South. In South Carolina, bleached sea-shells, broken crockery and glassware, broken pitchers, soap-dishes, lamp chimneys, tureens, coffee-cups, syrup jugs, all sorts of ornamental vases, cigar boxes, gun locks, tomato cans, teapots, flower pots, bits of stucco, plaster images, pieces of carved stone-work from one of the public buildings during the war, glass lamps and tumblers in great number, and forty other kitchen articles are used. On the children's graves were dolls' heads, little china wash-bowls and pitchers, toy images of animals, china vases, pewter dishes and other things which would interest a child.

Puckett, N. (1926). Folk Beliefs of the Southern Negro, p. 105

is dead and buried doesn't mean they have transformed into pure light. On the contrary, we must assume that spirits are just as they died, unless and until they have been elevated through the rituals of the living, or by receiving guidance from helper spirits in that realm. We have no way of knowing if evil people have been prayed for and forgiven, but we may know if they haven't been because troublesome people are troublesome spirits. They are opportunistic and will attach to you and wreak havoc in your life and in the lives of those around you if certain precautions are not observed.

Contrary to popular opinion, not all graveyard work is death work. That is like saying the Death card of the tarot only means the death of a person when seen in a layout. Bad habits can be buried in a graveyard, and dirt from a grave can be used for gambling luck, love and protection. Transformational work can be done in a graveyard. In New Orleans, it is not uncommon at all to find a Voodooist doing love conjure in a graveyard with the help of Baron Samedi, the loa of death and sexuality. There are many examples of these kinds of alternative works documented in Harry Middleton Hyatt's (1970) seminal work *Hoodoo-Conjuration-Rootwork-Witchcraft* and Niles Puckett's (1926) *Folk Beliefs of the American Negro,* for example. Don't let the word "graveyard" limit you to what can be accomplished with the help of the spirits and a little graveyard dirt.

In this book, we talk about many aspects of graveyard work primarily in the context of Southern Hoodoo and Rootwork. Working in the boneyard, and especially the practice of hiring spirits, should not be taken lightly. It is always safest to work with the spirits of your direct ancestors whenever possible; that is, those ancestors who were good and kind to you when they were living. If you decide to commission the help of a stranger or a murderer to do your dirty work for example, problems are likely to follow, especially if you do not observe the specific precautions described in the following chapters. Some spirits are just looking for a free ride out of the cemetery so they can proceed with activity consistent with their own agenda, as opposed to yours.

Graveyard work has a definite place in hoodoo; but, it's place is not necessarily with you and your personal practice. If you are new to this kind of work, ideally you can work under the tutelage of a more experienced rootworker. You need to be spiritually fit and protected. How ever you decide to proceed, you are advised to do so with caution and respect. If you are not sure about doing graveyard work, perhaps it is best if you don't.

CHOOSING A CEMETERY

St. Louis #1 is the mother cemetery ... the Vieux Carré of the dead; as confused and closely packed a quarter as the living metropolis... ~ **Grace King, 1895**

Cemeteries hold tangible links to the past, to our ancestors and to the spirit world. For this reason, rootworkers who incorporate graveyard work in their practice have one or two cemeteries where they do most of their work. They are very familiar with the layouts, the kind of cemeteries they are and who is buried there. It is a good idea to do some research on a cemetery before choosing it as a place for conjure work, if for no other reason than each cemetery has its own unique story to tell. The most important thing—all practical considerations aside—is that you feel comfortable when you are working there.

TYPES OF CEMETERIES

There are several different types of cemeteries which are designated public or private. Knowing the differences can help in locating specific dirts and spirits for specific conjure work. For example, national cemeteries will have military personnel buried in them. Also, learn the cemetery laws the state you are searching as laws differ between states.

1. City and County. Most city and county cemeteries date back to approximately 1850. Many date to the time of state registration.
2. Church. These are the most common type of cemetery, both in America and Europe. Burial registers are akin to Sexton's records and can be helpful in locating a specific person's grave. In recent times, churches have indexed their cemeteries by indexing the tombstones. Graves without tombstones are not recorded.
3. Family. Family cemeteries are abundant in the Eastern and Southern United States. They also exist in foreign countries. The only record of who is buried there other than tombstones and oral family history would be the record in a family bible, if one exists.
4. National. This is where you will find people who served in the military. National cemeteries always have caretakers and the office of the person in charge of the cemetery and its records in called a Sexton. Because of the sheer size of national cemeteries, you will need the Sexton's records to find specific plots.
5. Private. Private cemeteries are only used by a family or small portion of the local community.

LOCATING ANCESTRAL GRAVES

Using dirt obtained from the grave of an ancestor makes for powerful conjure. Some folks are fortunate enough to know where their ancestors are buried. If you do not have that information, there are a number of ways to find it.

First, you need to decide on whose grave it is you wish to locate. Once you decide which ancestor you want to find, you need to locate the correct cemeteries. Obituaries and death certificates typically document the place of internment. They can also provide you with the date of death and the date of the funeral and burial. In addition, they can provide information about your ancestor's name, place and year of birth, the names of their children, where they lived, their place in the family's birth order, names of towns and how long they lived in each one, the age of a spouse at death, details of the longevity of parents and grandparents, and a count of descendents by generation.

If you do not know the specific cemetery of entombment but you do know the town or county where a relative died, this is a great start. Try to determine where the family lived when the relatives you are looking for died. Census records and land deeds will usually identify the town or township of residence. Probates and church records may also provide this important information.

Once you have located the specific residence where your ancestor lived, make a list of cemeteries in that area. The internet is a treasure trove of information in this regard. You may want to call an organization in a county who would know about the cemeteries, such as county historical societies, mortuaries and funeral homes. Don't neglect to obtain print directories as they are still the best place to begin your search.

Three nationwide directories that can help identify existing cemeteries are:

1. *Cemeteries of the U.S.: A Guide to Contact Inform-*

ation for U.S. Cemeteries and their Records (1994) edited by Deborah M. Burek, Detroit: Gale Research Inc.
2. Elizabeth, G. and James, D. K. (1994). *United States Cemetery Address Book: All States, More Than 25,000 Cemeteries, Addresses, Locations.* Vallejo, Ca.: Indices Publishing.
3. *Geographic Names Information System* (GNIS), developed by the U.S. Geographical Survey.:
http://geonames.usgs.gov/domestic/

Some internet sources to help with locating ancestor graves include:

1. **USGenWeb**. Find links to all state genealogy websites which provide information to specific counties.
http://usgenweb.org/
2. **Cemetery Junction**. This site includes a list of more than 42,000 U.S. cemeteries, some of which have links to inscriptions elsewhere on-line.
http://www.daddezio.com/cemetery/

For on-line sources for locating Funeral Homes:

1. **FuneralNet.** Check out their Consumer Resources section for funeral home search, cemetery search and obituaries. http://www.funeralnet.com/index.php
2. **U.S. Funerals Online.** The directory names each funeral home and splits into states and then cities, and is arranged into Zip code order.
http://www.us-funerals.com/funeral-homes.html

Grave of Uncle Joe; died 1888; tombstone erected by B.J. Hoole, son-in-law of General John L. Hunter; "In memory of a trusted slave who continued as a servant after he was freed"; Fairview Cemetery, Eufaula, Alabama. Photo taken between 1930–1940 as part of the Federal Writer's project, p.d.

READING GRAVESTONE SIGNS AND SYMBOLS

"Invoked or not invoked, God will be present."
~ Epitaph of Carl Jung, 1875-1961

In each cemetery you visit, look for signs, symbols, and other information on the tombstones. These signs and symbols will give you a lot of information about the people who are buried there, as well as the people who buried them. You may find signs and symbols of occupations and affiliations of the deceased. Observe names and surnames on the gravestones and see if you recognize any that are the same as places, streets, and businesses in your town. Notice the different countries or states of birth listed on tombstones. This can tell you where most of the people in your area come from. All of these signs and symbols and the information derived from them can be extremely helpful when looking for a particular grave type.

Some of commonly found gravestone signs and symbols and their meanings are listed on the following pages.

ANIMALS

Bees: Resurrection; resurrection of Christ.
Birds: Souls; flight of the soul back to the Creator.
Birds in flight: Originating from ancient Egypt representing the "winged soul"; eternal life. Frequently seen on the graves of children.
Butterfly: The soul, occasionally seen on children's graves signifying a short life. It is symbolic of the resurrection of Christ and the three stages of life (caterpillar), death (chrysalis) and resurrection (butterfly).
Descending dove: Holy Ghost.
Dog: Represents loyalty and a person worth loving.
Dove: Peace; innocence; purity.
Dragon: Depicts good over evil as in St. George slaying the dragon.
Eagle: Courage and possibly a military career; symbol for Saint John.
Fish: Faith; Jesus Christ
Frog: Depicts sin, indulgence and worldly pleasure; alternately, may represent resurrection.
Horse: Courage or generosity. Horses are associated with St. George, St. Martin, St. Maurice and St. Victor, all of whom are represented in Christian iconography on horseback.
Lamb: Innocence, meekness, gentleness and humility; Christ the Redeemer. The lamb is the most common animal symbol found on a child's grave. It appears throughout the ages with great regularity in Christian art because it is a symbol of Christ (Croton Friends of History, n.d.).
Lion: Guardian of tombs against evil and bothersome spirits; symbolizes the power of God.

Owl: Wisdom.
Peacock: Symbolizes resurrection, beauty of soul, and immortality.
Phoenix: Same as *peacock*.
Serpent: Represents eternity when swallowing its own tail.
Rooster: Awakening, the Resurrection.
Squirrel with a nut: Religious meditation or spiritual striving.
Swallow: Indicates a child or motherhood.

BODY PARTS

Arms outstretched: Represents a plea for mercy.

Statuette of an Owl by a grave in the Midwest. Photo copyright 2008 Denise Alvarado, All rights reserved.

Eye of God/All-Seeing Eye: Symbolizes the all-knowing and ever-present God.
Hands: Symbol of leaving, devotion, prayer.
Hands, clasped: Symbol of piety; attention towards heaven.
Hands holding a chain with a broken link: Symbolizes the death of a family member.
Hands holding a heart: Charity, common on 19th century memorials. Often seen on memorials of members of the Independent Order of Odd Fellows.
Hands holding an open book: The embodiment of faith.
Hand pointing downward: Mortality or sudden death.

Thought to represent a secret Masonic handshake.
Hand pointing upward: Consequence of righteous living; heavenly reward.
Hands praying: Signifies devotion.
Heart: Love, mortality, love of God, courage and intelligence.
Heart, bleeding: Christ's suffering.
Heart encircled with thorns: Christ's suffering.
Heart, flaming: Symbolizes religious fervor.
Heart pierced by a sword: Represents the Virgin Mary; charity.

Gravestone in the Midwest, Photo copyright 2012 Denise Alvarado, All rights reserved.

OBJECTS/OTHER

Anchor: Hope; life eternal; may signify seafaring profession and/or St. Nicolas, patron saint of seamen.
Angel: Messenger of God; guardian angel; St. Michael is depicted with a sword while St. Gabriel is depicted with a horn.
Anvil: Martyrdom.
Arch: Triumph over death; victory.
Bible: Resurrection through scripture; wisdom.
Circle: Symbol of eternity and never-ending existence. Two circles, one above the other, represent earth and sky. Three interconnected circles represent the Holy Trinity.
Crossed keys: St. Peter.

Magnolia Cemetery, Mobile, Alabama. Photograph 1946, Carol Highsmith, public domain.

Cross: Salvation, love, faith and goodness.
Drapery over anything: Sorrow, grief, mourning.
Menorah: Jewish symbol for divine presence of God; represents the seven days for the creation of the world (The Cemetery Club, n.d.).
Pyramid: Eternity. It was believed that a pyramid-shaped tombstone prevented the devil from reclining on a grave (The Cemetery Club, n. d.).

Rising sun: Resurrection; life.
Rock: Steadfastness, stability; also a symbol of St. Peter.
Shell: Pilgrimage; baptism of Christ; resurrection.
Skull: Death; sin.
Setting sun: Death.
Star, five-pointed: Symbolizes the life of Jesus.
Star, Five-pointed pentagram: Known by pre-Christian Celtic priests as the Witch's Foot; also known as Solomon's Seal and the Goblin's Cross. Popular among demonologists and believed to have protective powers against evil. To the Jews, it represents the five mosaic books. This symbol was adopted by Masonic organizations.
The Star of David: Symbol of Judaism, the Star of David is made of two triangles and signifies divine protection.

TREES AND PLANTS

Bouquets: Condolences; grief.
Buds: Renewal of life; if broken, a life cut short.
Cedar: Strong faith.
Flower: Brevity of earthly existence; sorrow; premature death.
Ivy: Enduring memory; friendship
Lilies: Resurrection; purity; associated with the Virgin Mary and Archangel Gabriel.
Oak: Supernatural power and strength; eternity
Roses: Beauty, love, purity.
Tree: The Tree of Life; faith.
Tree trunk: Premature death.
Willow: Sorrow, weeping; grief.
Wreath: Eternity; victory in death.

Forgotten grave in Arizona. Photo copyright 2012, Denise Alvarado, All rights reserved.

GRAVESTONE RUBBINGS

"The only real equality is in the cemetery."
~ German proverb

In addition to collecting graveyard dirt, you may want to procure a rubbing of the tombstone from which you gathered the dirt. The rubbing can be kept in the jar or bag where you store the dirt and can be placed under a candle used in a work that calls upon the spirit hired as a link to that spirit. In the case of a gravestone rubbing from an ancestral grave, the rubbing can be framed and kept on the ancestral altar as a unique memento.

Gravestone rubbing is controversial and banned in some cemeteries, often due to restoration projects. Should you decide to try a get a rubbing from a tombstone, here are a few things to consider:

1. Check to see if rubbing is allowed in the cemetery and get the proper permit if needed.
2. Avoid rubbing rough, eroded or damaged stones and stones on which there is lichen.
3. You will not be able to get a rubbing from every gravestone. Only a sharp stone carving will yield a good

clean print. The paper often tears when rubbings are attempted on rounded, high relief carvings.
4. Use paper that is much larger than the gravestone and attach it to the stone with masking tape. Don't forget to bring a pair of scissors to cut your paper for smaller stones.
5. Masking tape comes off of paper easily and will not leave any marks on the gravestone.
6. While any kind of paper can be used, experts recommend a synthetic rice paper called Aqaba, a dress making fabric called Pellon, or even meat wrapping paper.
7. For the actual rubbing, use a thick crayon. Try not to use something like charcoal or pastels as these have the tendency to smear. If you do use charcoal, chalk or pastels, you may want to spray your rubbing as soon as possible with a sealer to prevent smearing. Sealers can be found at any art or hobby store.
8. For the best result, use long, flat strokes when rubbing and avoid rubbing in all different directions with different strokes. Concentrate along the edges of the raised portions to bring out the detail. If you are rubbing the entire stone, be sure to get the edges so you can see the shape of the stone.

Finally, don't forget to write down any details about the grave on the reverse side of the paper (or on a separate piece of paper if you prefer) for future reference.

GRAVEYARD ETIQUETTE

"It is a common practice to bring dirt from a man's burial place if he died far away from home, or better, to bring a piece of his clothes. Thus, the returning spirit will find he has not been neglected by his family, and will therefore be disinclined to trouble them with sickness and misfortune." ~ Niles Puckett, 1926

Trample on the dust of the dead lightly...is a sentiment held by old timers. The saying is a subtle reminder of the importance of observing certain behaviors while in a graveyard. For example, be careful where you walk. Don't step on graves or sit on tombstones. Not only is it just rude and inconsiderate, it is a violation of the deceased's personal space. Always ask before taking anything—even stones, flowers, sticks and leaves. Never leave trash, always greet the gatekeeper and if you ever get a bad feeling, leave immediately. The important thing to remember is that when working in the boneyard you never just walk in and take something. You must always treat the spirits with respect; both the spirits of the deceased, as well as the guardians of the cemeteries and the psychopomps.

Proper graveyard etiquette is of the utmost importance

because we don't know what kinds of preparations or customs were observed in the burials of the deceased. Some folks of earlier days held many taboos surrounding the treatment of dying and dead people. If offended, it was believed that the spirits of the dead might return to cause great mischief. One took special care to avoid contact with ghosts, using both disguise and such propitiations as gifts or flattery. Proper burial procedures, however, would prevent the restless dead from haunting the living (Graham, n.d.). Even the most callous of unbelievers "hesitate to take liberties with burial-places for fear of incurring the wrath of supernatural powers, not the least terrible because they were undefined" (Puckle, 1926).

Cemeteries are alive with spirits and haints. Just as proper burial procedures are said to prevent hauntings, proper graveyard etiquette will do the same. Many spirits just linger around; some will attach themselves to you while you collect dirt if you are not careful, particularly if certain precautions are not taken.

Following are some suggestions for entering and leaving a cemetery. These are merely suggestions—they are what we find works for us and for other rootworkers we know. If you have someone teaching you, they may have a different way of doing things. You should do whatever feels right to you; the important thing is that you do some sort of act of reverence and respect when entering and leaving the cemetery.

ENTERING AND LEAVING

There are different ways to enter a cemetery. One way is to stand at the entrance and ask for permission to enter. If you feel any kind of discomfort or bad vibes, leave and come back another day. If you feel every thing is fine, pour rum on the ground 3 times and enter. Luisah Teish suggests another way to enter the cemetery is to stand at the entrance and knock three times while asking to enter. If the energy feels right, leave three pennies at the gate and enter (Teish, personal communication, 2012).

Leaving a cemetery is just as important as entering. When you are ready to leave, pour some rum on the ground and back out of the cemetery. Thank the gatekeeper. Always go home a different way than you came. When you get home, take a cleansing bath of salt and lavender. This will remove any spiritual hitchhikers that may have followed you home.

In summary, here are a few techniques you can do to prevent any unwanted backlash from your cemetery visits:

1. Always approach a cemetery with respect.
2. Always greet the guardian of the cemetery. Knock 3 times before entering and leave 3 pennies at the gate.
3. Be sure to pay for the dirt you take.
4. Go home a different way from whence you came.
5. As a matter of precaution, turn around three times before entering your home after visiting a graveyard to confuse the spirits.
6. Take a spiritual cleansing bath upon returning home to prevent unwanted ghostly attachments.

Following the above suggestions will help ensure success in your graveyard work.

THE HAUNTED NEW ORLEANS WISHING TOMB

Tomb of Marie Laveau, St. Louis Cemetery 1, New Orleans. Photo 2006, Patrick S. Carroll, p.d.

Our destiny changes with our thought; we shall become what we wish to become, do what we wish to do, when our habitual thought corresponds with our desire.
~ Orison Swett Marden

A book about working in cemeteries in the context of Southern Hoodoo would not be complete without some mention of the infamous Wishing Tomb in St. Louis Cemetery #1, the oldest graveyard in New Orleans, Louisiana. This is the tomb where the reigning Voodoo Queen of New Orleans Marie Laveau reportedly rests. Her tomb has become a pilgrimage site for Voodooists and others interested in paying homage to the infamous Voodoo Queen.

Ancestor reverence is at the foundation of New Orleans Voodoo. When Marie Laveau was alive, people would go to her home on St. Ann Street and knock at her door to ask for help. In death, people go to her new home—her grave site—to knock and ask for help.

Indeed, the magickal properties ascribed to Marie Laveau's final resting place is one of the most intriguing pieces of New Orleans folklore. Miracles have reportedly occurred after performing the rite associated with the tomb. The most remarkable story is of a Missouri woman who won two million dollars in the state lottery after reportedly making her wish there.

There is some disagreement as to whether or not the tomb is actually the resting place of Marie Laveau. There is also the question of which Marie Laveau—I or II—is buried there. Her obituary states that she was buried in the Glapion family tomb in St. Louis Cemetery No. 1. The first two lines of the inscription on the Laveau-Glapion tomb read, "Famille Vve. Paris/ née Laveau." *Vve.* is an abbreviation for *Veuve,* (Widow); thus, the phrase translates, "Family of the Widow Paris, born Laveau" (Marie Laveau I). This appears to be evidence that the tomb is indeed hers and that conjectures to the contrary simply fuel her mythos and mystique. That said, it does not explain the other seemingly forgotten grave in one of the oven walls in St. Louis Cemetery #2 that also has her name on it.

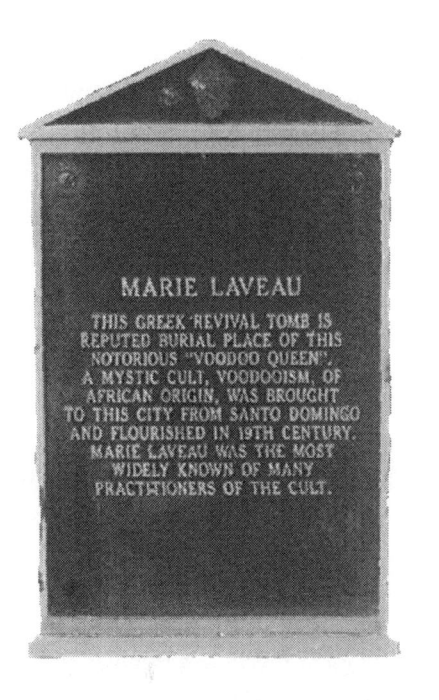

On any given day, the Laveau-Glapion tomb can be found with a cornucopia of gifts on the ground next to it. People customarily leave coins, Mardi Gras beads and doubloons, candles, Voodoo dolls, gris gris, flowers and written letters, and a host of other things. The tomb is almost always covered with graffiti consisting mostly of X's written with pieces of broken red brick confiscated from neighboring tombs. People make a wish as they draw their red cross marks.

There are a number of versions of the actual ritual for making the wish. One version entails people knocking on the tomb three times and making their wish while drawing three crossmarks. Sometimes, people will also turn around three times after doing so. In his book *Voodoo in New Orleans*, Robert Tallant (1946) described people bringing flowers, burning candles and leaving pennies and nickels in the green flower-holders that were attached to each side of the tomb. According to Jim Haskins (1990), the ritual consists of drawing the X, placing your hand over it, rubbing your foot three times against the bottom of the tomb, throwing some silver coins into the cup, and then making your wish.

To find the tomb of Marie Laveau in St. Louis Cemetery #1, enter the cemetery at the front gate. Turn left and count between the 5th and 6th tombs on your right and walk through the space between the two tombs. Look up at about 11:00 o'clock and there it is!

THE CAMPAIGN TO PROTECT THE TOMB OF MARIE LAVEAU

In 2005, Save Our Cemeteries (S.O.C.), the Tour Guide Association of Greater New Orleans (TGAGNOI) and the New Orleans Archdiocesan Cemeteries joined forces in a campaign to stop the desecration of Marie Laveau's tomb in St. Louis Cemetery No. 1. Visitors to St. Louis No. 1

have been desecrating the Glapion family tomb for years now by marking it with crossmarks using broken red bricks from nearby graves and leaving inappropriate offerings at the foot of the tomb. These actions are illegal and are not part of any traditional New Orleans Voodoo rite. Furthermore, it adversely affects other tombs in the area when bricks are taken from them to make the typical three X's.

According to Save Our Cemeteries, Inc. (2005), the tomb was washed with lime, restoring it to a white finish. Two signs were posted that state: "Marking on tombs, removing any artifact from this cemetery or any act of vandalism, defacement or damage carried out on this premises will be aggressively prosecuted under city ordinance Section 54-377, 38-11, 38-12 and State Law RS 14: 225." The organization has actively encouraged members of the hospitality and tourism industries to educate people on the laws pertaining to the desecration of grave sites in New Orleans.

Despite ongoing efforts to prevent the defacing of Marie Laveau's tomb, people still engage in the practice and the tomb has to be periodically whitewashed and cleansed.

THE WISHING RITUAL

As an alternative to the active defacement of Marie Laveau's tomb and as a way to have access to the Wishing Tomb at all times, you may use a photograph of her tomb. Using the principles of sympathetic magic, you can interact with the photograph—which serves as a sympathetic link from the physical world to the spirit world—to make your crossmarks and petition the great Voodoo Queen.

First, put an image of her tomb in a frame and set it on an altar created for her. Using a red lipstick, mark 3 Xs on the tomb side by side (XXX). Knock on the photo 3 times and ask Marie Laveau out loud to grant your wish. For example, "Beautiful Marie Laveau, miracle worker of the courts, please see that the judge rules in my favor in my court case". Then turn around three times counterclockwise, light a blue candle, and make an offering of fresh flowers, coconut cake or fruit.

Scan the QR code with your smart phone or Android to find a photograph of Marie Laveau's tomb.

When your wish comes true, wipe off the crossmarks and clean the frame as if tidying up her grave. Thank Mam'zelle and make a donation to charity in her honor. Repeat as needed

XXX

BUYING GRAVEYARD DIRT

Grave dust is what a witch uses to hoodoo you and you will conquer her if you get some and wear it.
~African American, 1926

Graveyard dirt is a staple ingredient in the medicine/medzin chest of any rootworker, especially in New Orleans. It is used in many, many types of spells, from spells of justice to spells of revenge, love and gambling. There are also death spells where it is employed; however, its use for this reason is the least common. Any reference to such work in this book is given for its folkloric value and educational purposes only.

There is nothing complicated about graveyard dirt. Graveyard dirt is not code for some secret herbal blend—it is quite simply, dirt from a graveyard. The means of collecting graveyard dirt is what gives it it's power. Grave dirt is dirt collected from an actual grave. Grave dirt is always purchased from the spirit of the deceased who lies in the grave. A magical contract is made with the spirit and the dirt is usually paid for with coins and rum or whiskey. Graveyard dirt is purchased from the guardian of the cemetery and gathered from the general cemetery grounds. Nine pennies, fifteen cents and a silver dime are

Freshly dug grave in a cemetery in Iowa. Photograph Copyright 2012, Denise Alvarado.

common coin combinations offered as payment for graveyard dirt.

Offering coins as a means of payment has its roots in African traditions. Coins were placed in the eyes of the deceased to keep them closed. They were placed in the palms of the deceased to represent their contribution to the ancestors, as well as for payment for crossing over in a good way. Coins were also placed around the gravesite for the same reasons. Clearly, a connection can be seen between this old custom and the ongoing practice of leaving money at the gravesite as payment for services rendered.

One of the concerns people often express is how to gather graveyard dirt without being noticed. There are several ways this can be done. One way is to work at a cemetery that is not frequented often. Some of the old forgotten cemeteries are the best to work in as they are typically alive with spirits. If you don't do much work in the cemetery at all, then wait and go in the spring or summer or at All Saints Day and bring some flowers or a potted plant. Alternately, you can bring a plant to actually plant in the ground next to the headstone and when planting the plant, you can inconspicuously grab some dirt from the grave while you are at it.

Sometimes graveyard dirt is referred to as graveyard dust or goofer dust; however, these terms are not synonymous. Graveyard dust is the fine dirt and dust particles procured from off of the gravestones and surrounding cemetery. Goofer dust is something entirely different, though graveyard dirt is a component in goofer dust. Finally, graveyard dirt is not pulverized mullein or patchouli leaves as it is touted to be by some folks from outside the Hoodoo tradition.

HIRING A SPIRIT

When you collect dirt from a grave, you can hire the spirit of that grave to perform a job for you. Sometimes spirits will comply with your request and other times they won't. This can be a dangerous activity if you don't know what you are doing. Doing any kind of work in a graveyard requires mindful intention, especially when hiring a spirit to assist you in a given work.

Spirits can be hired for a single basis work or for multiple workings. A good rule of thumb is to get to know the spirit before hiring it. Do some research on the spirit by looking into the history of the cemetery and the various people buried there. Take some time to walk around and observe the signs and symbols. Take note of the epitaphs. Epitaphs can be significant sources of information about who is buried in a given grave. Epitaphs are essentially the final chance to formally communicate with the world something of importance about the deceased. Sometimes people write their own epitaphs before they die and it is their own words we read.

Certain information about the deceased can also be gleaned in the older cemeteries where African Americans and Native Americans are buried by noting the position of the grave in relation to the rest of the cemetery or in relation to the cardinal directions. For example, graves facing North/South apparently indicate that the deceased died under mysterious circumstances. Seeing a grave situated in this manner means the spirit cannot rest comfortably until the cause of death is determined and retribution is achieved.

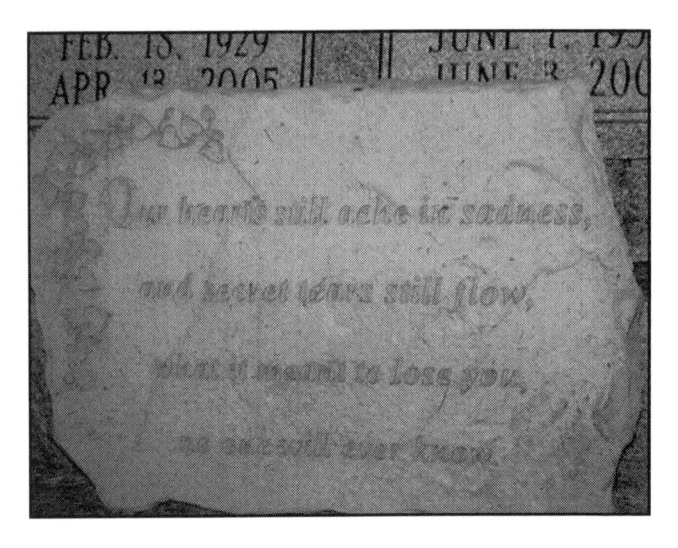

When you are canvassing the cemetery in search of a specific grave, take some offerings of food, flowers and whiskey or rum with you to the graveyard. If you know a particular spirit was a teetotaler, leave out the alcohol. You may also want to bring a candle and walk around the graveyard by candlelight if you are working at night. As you approach a grave, set the candle down and meditate for a few moments. Ask the spirit if it is willing to do the work you ask. Listen quietly for your answer. If they agree, tell them exactly what you want them to do. Tell them what you will pay them for the work. After you have reached an agreement with the spirit, proceed with taking a little dirt from the head, heart and foot of the grave. It is only necessary to dig a couple of inches deep. We have heard tell of some old timers digging up to the elbow before collecting the dirt, but most people we know only go a couple of inches deep.

As payment for the dirt you collect, leave a silver dime in the holes from which you get the dirt, and then cover up the holes. In the absence of a silver or mercury dime, a regular dime will do. If it is needed and you are so inclined, take some time to tidy up the grave. If there are weeds growing up around the grave pull them, and if there is dirt on the gravestone brush it clean (into a little medicine bottle and you've got yourself some graveyard dust). Depending on what you are asking of the Spirit, you may want to leave some flowers and a little bottle of rum at the gravesite.

Some conjurers offer a dime to the entire cemetery and all of its inhabitants; others just leave it at the one grave where the dirt was collected. If you are collecting dirt from the cemetery at large and not a specific grave, leaving your offering at the gates for the entire cemetery and its inhabitants is appropriate. You may also place the dime into the hole you dug to get your dirt and then cover it up. Dirt from a graveyard in general can be used to add earth energy to mojos and gris gris, to fix candles or to bring forth the energy of the dead in any work. In the African traditional religions, graveyard dirt is often use as an offering to specific spirits such as Oya, who is the Guardian of the Cemeteries.

Whatever you do, be sure to thank the spirit of the grave and leave the cemetery going a different way from whence you came. If you see some old flower pieces or leaves that have obviously been blown from an unknown grave, pick those up as well. Graveyard ephemeron is one of our favorite bonus conjure items to score in a cemetery. Just don't forget to thank the spirits for the lagniappe!

Once you get home, dry out any dirt you may have gathered by spreading it out on paper bags. Once it is dry, you can sift it to remove any critters or rocks and twigs, then bag and mark it for the task it was gathered for. Save the bigger pieces for use in bottle spells and mojo bags.

There are many variations on the general themes presented here and there are a number of other considerations in the collection of graveyard dirt. For example, the time of day, moon phase, and type of grave are considerations, as are the specific types of graves from which the dirt is gathered.

Grave-digger, 1871. Viktor Vasnetsov, p.d.

TIME AND MOON PHASE CORRESPONDANCES

"We have a star that is called Job, repisent Job in his coffin. It's complete - you kin see the shape of the coffin an' you kin see the form of Job. That is a star."

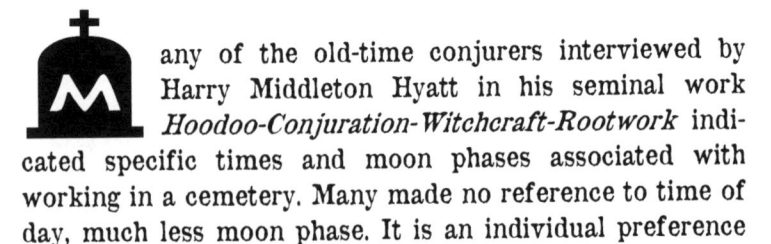

Many of the old-time conjurers interviewed by Harry Middleton Hyatt in his seminal work *Hoodoo-Conjuration-Witchcraft-Rootwork* indicated specific times and moon phases associated with working in a cemetery. Many made no reference to time of day, much less moon phase. It is an individual preference as to whether or not you will consider these conditions when doing your own graveyard work.

Following are some works that illustrate the variations and correspondences with regards to moon phase and time of day or night dirt is to be collected.

Nine o'clock at Night, North Side—To Steal a Husband from Another Woman

Here's a rather extreme way to go about stealing another woman's husband. Go to a graveyard at nine o'clock at night and get some dirt from a grave that is on the north side of the graveyard. Take it to the home of the woman who has the husband you want and sprinkle it around the house. It is ideal if you can sprinkle some around the woman's bed. When she walks over the dirt it will cause her to wither away and die, giving you the opportunity to get her man. [Memphis, Tenn., (1541), 2787:11.] From *Hoodoo-Conjuration-Witchcraft-Rootwork* Vol. 4 by Harry Middleton Hyatt.

Midnight, No Moon Shining—To Harm a Person; For Bad Luck

To cause someone to have bad luck, go to a graveyard at midnight when no moon is shining and get some graveyard dirt. Take that dirt and throw it at your enemy and they will never be successful in anything they do. [New Orleans, La. (866), 1403:2]. From *Hoodoo-Conjuration-Witchcraft-Rootwork* Vol. 4 by Harry Middleton Hyatt.

Midnight—For Good Luck and Success; to Call For the Spirits; To Find a Murderer; To Kill a Person

To be successful, go to a graveyard at midnight and buy some dirt from the grave of a successful person. Pay $1.25 and a bottle of rum for the dirt. Carry the dirt in a mojo bag with a High John the Conqueror root and some Solomon's seal and anoint the bag with Crown of Success oil.

One o'clock in the Morning—To Make a Person Move

Go to a cemetery at one o'clock in the morning and get

some dirt from a trucker's grave and pay him a quarter and a beer. Take that dirt and sprinkle it on the porch of the person you want to move and they will.

Four o'clock in the Morning—To Get a Raise; To Make a Person Leave

To make your boss give you a raise as well as to make him like you, go to a graveyard at four o'clock in the morning and buy some dirt from the head to the middle of a grave of someone. The informant mentions getting dirt from someone who carried a gun, but he also says it doesn't matter whose grave you get it from. Take that dirt and somehow get it on your boss and he will likely give you a raise and you will become good friends. [Brunswick, Ga., (1183), 1996:5]. From *Hoodoo-Conjuration-Witchcraft-Rootwork* Vol. 4 by Harry Middleton Hyatt.

Before Sunrise—To Keep Out Unwanted Persons

To keep unwanted people away, go to a graveyard before sunrise and get some graveyard dust using the three Holy names: *In the name of the Father, and of the Son and the Holy Ghost*. Take a penny and rub the penny with the graveyard dust until it is bright and shiny. Place the penny in your doorway to filter out the riff raff. [Florence, S. Car., (1320), 2264:2]. From *Hoodoo-Conjuration-Witchcraft-Rootwork* Vol. 5 by Harry Middleton Hyatt.

Before Sunrise—For Gambling Luck

For gambling luck, go to a graveyard before sunrise and get some dirt from the heart of a person's grave. Put some in your shoes or wrap it in a rag and put it in your pocket and it will bring you luck in gambling. [St. Petersburg, Fla.] From *Hoodoo-Conjuration-Witchcraft-Rootwork* Vol. 4 by Harry Middleton Hyatt.

Full Moon—To Bring in Customers

To draw customers to your place of business, go to a graveyard during a full moon and buy some dirt taken from a fresh grave. Mix the grave dirt with sulfur and red pepper and bury it under the front steps and it will bring in customers. [Sumter, N. Car] From *Hoodoo-Conjuration-Witchcraft-Rootwork* Vol. 4 by Harry Middleton Hyatt.

New Moon—To Keep Your Man from Following You When You Want to Go Out

If you are a woman and want to be able to go out and not be bothered by your man or partner following you, go to the graveyard on a new moon and get some dirt off an innocents grave. Mix it with sulfur and 9 spoons of table salt. Before leaving the house, go into your room and throw it around, and as you go out the door, toss some in the name of the Father, the Son, and the Holy Ghost, and go on your merry way. [Fayetteville, N. Car. (1423), 2563:2). From *Hoodoo-Conjuration-Witchcraft-Rootwork* Vol. 4 by Harry Middleton Hyatt.

GRAVE-TYPE CORRESPONDENCES

If de spirit take yo' misery an yo' troubles away
Well he goin' want somebody else to put it on.
He turn right round an' put it on yo'
Well if yo' ain't got sense nuff to protect yo'self
Why he'll take de misery offa de person yo' cure
An' bring it right back to yo'.
~ Doctor Yousee, Waycross, Georgia

Some works require specialized cemetery dirt for that dirt's specific qualities, such as dirt from the grave of a baby or a doctor. Sometimes, the manner in which the person died is of importance, as is how you collect the dirt in relation to the parts of the body. Some works call for dirt collected from the head of the grave, others from the heart or the feet.

If you need dirt to send somebody away (not kill them), dig your dirt at the head of an old grave. The oldest one in a cemetery works the best. For enemy works, dirt from the grave of a criminal is often used. People who engaged in unlawful behavior and questionable morals while living are more inclined to carry out left-handed works at the request of the worker; although, they are also more likely to go rogue on you which makes them dangerous to work with. Some love spells require dirt that you have gotten from the grave of a loved one such as a deceased spouse or relative. The loved one does not have to be a person, as even a beloved pet can be used for this purpose. Dirt dug from the grave of a hanged person or person who was executed is considered by many to be the most powerful for hexing and revenge magic.

When gathering graveyard dirt, it is helpful to note from whose grave you are gathering and the reasons for gathering it. Carry a pen and paper and write down the name of the cemetery and the person's name and date of birth and death so you have it for easy reference at a later date. For example:

Infant graveyard Dirt

Baby Donald Joseph 2 days old, 1965

Williams cemetery, Arizona

That way when you use the dirt later, you can call the spirit by name and thank them for helping you and allowing you to use the dirt from their grave.

Following is a list of types of graveyard spirits that can be hired. Spirits are identified by the different kinds of people buried in a cemetery and the various kinds of works that are done with dirt gathered from their specific graves. Refer to the Grave Type Correspondences chart on page 47 for a quick reference for the grave-type, the purpose for its use and where on the actual grave the dirt should be gathered.

Graveyard dirt that has been recorded, prepared and stored for future use. Photo copyright 2012 Denise Alvarado, All rights reserved.

Ancestor Grave

Dirt from the grave of an ancestor can be used on the ancestral altar in honor of their memory.

Baby's Grave

Dirt from the grave of a baby has historically had several correspondences including creating peace in the home, dispelling conflict, making someone move, making a lover return, making someone fall asleep, and keeping the law away. In addition, there are subcategories of graveyard dirt from babies including dirt from the grave of a baby that never cried, such as a stillborn baby.

Criminal's Grave

Dirt from a criminal's grave is used for enemy works, to cause confusion and to make folks argue. Caution: These spirits are not trustworthy and are best left alone.

Gambler's Grave

Gambler's grave dirt is used for luck in games of chance, the lottery and bingo.

Indian Grave

Dirt from the grave of a Native American must be done with the utmost respect or the spirits of the cemetery will follow you home and haunt you. And there is nothing like an angry Indian spirit to rock your world. One big rule is to never utter any name while in the cemetery because anyone with that name will think you are calling them and they will follow you as you leave. Dirt from an Indian grave is used for spells of defense, protection, and scouting (i.e. divining who is after you, who has fixed you, where your enemy is and what their next step is).

Doctor or Nurse's Grave
For spells of healing and good health, successful surgeries, finding cures.

Soldier's Grave
For spells of protection, domination and courage. When you need someone who will follow orders precisely and fight your battles for you.

Lawyer's Grave
For court cases, keeping the law away, staying out of jail keeping someone in jail, getting out of prison, divorce cases, child custody, all legal issues.

Murder Victims and the Unjustly Executed Graves
Death spells, vengeance. Working with murder victims and those who have been wrongly executed is potentially dangerous. Many times these spirits are stuck and require elevation so that they can literally rest in peace. If they are angry or vengeful, they may take it out on you if you are of a category (i.e. race, occupation, name, etc.) that is consistent with the murderer or executioner. On the other hand, these spirits may be employed as spirits of retribution. They may also be employed as spiritual advocates for others who may be suffering unjustly.

Table 1. Grave-type Correspondences

GRAVE-TYPE	PURPOSE	LOCATION
Ancestor	Ancestor reverence, memorial	Head, heart, foot
Banker	Money, financial independence	Both hands, head
Banker	Money, financial independence	Both hands, head
Criminal	Enemy work	Left hand
Doctor or nurse	Healing or causing illness	Both hands, head
Elderly person	Wisdom, patience	Head
Father	Protection, discipline	Head, hands
Gambler	Luck in games of chance, lottery, bingo	Right hand
Hoodoo person	power	Both hands, feet, head, heart
Indian	Defense, protection, scouting	Hands, fee, head, heart
Lawyer	Court cases	Both hands, head
Mother	Nurturing, healing, comfort, guidance	Heart, head hands
Murder victim	Death, vengeance	Head, heart
Musician	Improve musical skill, communication	Hands, heart
Policeman	Protection, detection, investigation	Both hands, feet
Soldier	Protection, removal of enemies	Both hands, feet
Spiritual leader	Spiritual guidance and advice	heart
Teacher	Improve thinking and learning, cognitive ability	head
Unjustly executed	Justice, retribution	Left hand
Wealthy person	money	Both hands, head

GRAVEYARD WORKS

Be peaceful, be courteous, obey the law, respect everyone; but if someone puts his hand on you, send him to the cemetery.
~ Malcolm X

Graveyard dirt is traditionally used in many ways. It is used for ancestor reverence, protection spells, coercive love spells, court case spells, harming and enemy tricks. Graveyard dirt is kept on altars of various spirits having to do with the dead. It is also kept on ancestral altars (particularly if the dirt is from the grave of an ancestor), and it is kept in prendas (Palo) and spirit pots (New Orleans Voodoo).

The following works all involve going to a graveyard and gathering dirt of various kinds. Since the previous sections covered how to do this, cemetery protocol is not repeated in every work. When the work calls for going to a cemetery, it is assumed you will do so according to the guidelines already described.

To Make a Roommate Move

To make a roommate move, gather some graveyard dirt from a baby's grave and mix with dirt dauber's nest. Sprinkle it in the bedroom of the roommate, preferably around the bed and in a dark corner. It is said that the spirit of the baby will cry and haunt the person, terrifying them so much they will move.

To Get Rid of Someone

If you have been fighting with your partner and want him or her gone, go to a cemetery and walk around the various tombs and gather some dust from several graves until you have a handful. Be sure to leave a dime at each grave you dust off as payment. Take that dust and after they have gone to sleep, put some in the pair of shoes they wear most often. It is believed that as their feet sweat, the dust will absorb into their skin and make the person shrivel up and whither away or simply leave.

To Make Your Business Grow

To make your business grow, buy some grave dirt from the grave of a successful businessman or woman and toss it in all four corners of your home as well as across the threshold of your front door.

To Attract a Lover

Go to a cemetery and gather grave dirt from the heart area of a person of the same sex you wish to attract. If you know the person, all the better. On a piece of red paper, write the name of the person you wish to attract, and then write your name on top of theirs. Add some vandal root and a pinch of Vetivert along with a pinch of the graveyard dirt you just gathered and wrap it all up in a little paper package, taking care to fold the paper towards you when closing. Tie with a piece of string and place under your mattress.

To Keep Someone in Jail

Gather some grave dirt from a lawyer, a judge or police officer's grave and dirt from a court house and a police station (3 dirts altogether). Mix all 3 dirts together with ground chicory root. Place a photo of the person you want to stay in jail or prison on a red plate and sprinkle with the graveyard dirt blend. Burn a black 7 day candle that has been fixed with *Domination* oil by the plate (for the formula for Domination oil, see the section *Formulas*). On the 8th day, wrap the items in a black cloth and bury under a tree in a cemetery.

Graveyard Protection Jar

Place the following in a wooden bowl by the light of a white candle and a black candle:

- Palo Muerto
- Red Chili Powder
- Black Pepper Corns
- Dirt from 9 Cemeteries
- 9 old pennies

Mix well and place in a brown paper bag. Carefully roll the bag to close it. Bury the bag in a cemetery for 9 days. Leave offerings for the Dead when you retrieve it. Place the mixture in a clean dark jar (the ones yeast come in are perfect for this) along with a piece of amethyst. Sprinkle some of the mixture near you when conjuring and ask the Dead for their protection.

For a Peaceful Home

For a peaceful home, go to a graveyard and get dirt from the grave of a person known to have lived a righteous life. Sprinkle it in and around your house and your home will be peaceful from that point forward.

Cemetery Money Spell

Take a wooden box and place 3 gold coins, dirt from a rich person's grave and some saffron inside. Take this to the biggest tree in the cemetery. Bury for 3 days. Retrieve the box on the third day and leave some fruit and vegetables under the tree. Place the gold coins on your money altar for a boost in finances and eliminating debt. Use the grave dirt and saffron as a floor sprinkle to draw money or add to a money mojo bag.

Gravestone Dust for Good Luck

Locate the grave of a person of means. Preferably this will be an older headstone. If you don't know of any, you will need to sit quietly in the cemetery for awhile and ask the spirits to guide you. Once you have located the grave, take a chip off of the gravestone itself. Pay the spirit with 15 cents and a small bottle of rum. Using a knife, scrape the left side of the gravestone chip towards you making gravestone dust. As you are scraping the dust say "Lord let there be luck" three times. Put the gravestone dust in a red flannel bag and tie it around your waist for good luck playing the lottery and numbers.

To Cut Something from Your Life

Write on brown paper what you want removed from your life. Cut the paper into little pieces. Place these into a black bag along with 9 old pennies under the first tree in the cemetery. Do this under a dark moon. Walk away and don't look back.

To Stop an Enemy

Take 9 cherimoya seeds and tie them into a black cloth along with your enemy's photo. Tie the bundle with black thread. Take the bundle to the cemetery at midnight and bury it, cursing your enemy as you bury the bundle. This will reportedly poison the enemy's life.

Chimoya fruit and seeds from Central America. The fruit is edible but the seeds are highly toxic. They can be found in most Asian and international markets.

Oya War Water (Santeria)

Take a large glass jar to the cemetery just before a storm. Bury the jar half way in the ground with the lid off. After the storm, retrieve the jar and leave an offering of eggplant and sangria. When you return home, add 9 nails to whatever is in the jar. Place the lid back on the jar and put in a dark place for 9 days. Sprinkle some of this water in the path of your enemy or splash some on their front door.

Graveyard Charm for Protection

Gather three pieces of Sampson Snakeroot and three pieces of Blacksnake root and cut them the size of your right index finger. Using red cotton thread weave the 6 roots together, going under and over until they are secure. Then, fold them over so you have three on top of three, and tie them together. Put in a leather bag with a pinch of graveyard dirt. Carry it with you for protection and good luck.

Way back in slavery time that was luck to keep yo' boss from whuppin' yo'. Ole people carried dat - dat's all dey had to pertek deyself.

To Break Up a Couple

To break up a couple, put some graveyard dirt, aloes powder, salt, pepper and nine needles into a bottle. Then, take a lemon and write the couple's names on the lemon nine times and stick it into the bottle. Shake the bottle up real good and bury it in a graveyard. It is said the couple will break up in a bitter feud.

Enemy Jar Spell

To exact revenge on an enemy, make this Enemy Jar Spell. You will need:

- 1 empty clean jar
- Goats milk
- White vinegar
- Wasp nest
- Cayenne pepper
- Black pepper
- Photo of enemy

Roll the photo into a tube, rolling away from you. Secure with 9 straight pins, making sure the head of the pin is towards you. Drop this in the jar. Add the wasp nest and peppers. Add the vinegar, then the goats milk. Don't fill the jar all the way. Put the lid on and give it a good shake. Burn a black candle for 9 days, giving the jar a shake every time you light the candle and curse your enemy. After 9 days, take the jar to the back of an old cemetery. Dig a hole and place the jar upside down in the hole and fill the hole up. Walk away and don't look back. Cleanse yourself with a lavender and salt bath when you get home.

To Keep Your Boss In Line

Write your boss's name on a piece of brown paper sack. Write your name over it 9 times. Roll the paper toward you and tie with red thread. Bury in a cemetery with white sugar and a silver dime.

Beef Tongue Curse

Take a beef tongue and split it down the middle but not all the way through. Write your enemies name on a piece of brown paper sack. Fold it away from you 3 times. Place your paper in the split of the beef tongue. Sprinkle with cayenne pepper and salt. Add 9 chili's and 9 cherimoya seeds. Close the tongue by pushing it together and tying it with rope or twine. Wrap the fixed tongue in black cloth and bury it in the back of the cemetery. Say a curse and walk away.

Graveyard Gambling Mojo

Go to the grave of a known alcoholic and dig at the heart of the grave until you get to clay. Grab a handful of the clay and leave 15 cents as payment for the spirit. Bring the grave clay home and soak it in Hoyt's cologne. Spread it out on newspaper for a few days to allow it to dry out. Then, using a mortar and pestle grind the clay to a fine powder and put some in a bag made of leather or chamois cloth. Keep that bag in your pocket and before gambling, dust some of it on your hands and rub your hands together briskly. Throughout the game, touch the mojo in your pocket any time you feel the need to recharge your luck.

81 Knot Gambling Mojo

Take a red flannel bag and turn it inside out. Using both strings that you tie the mojo bag with, tie 9 knots. You have to leave the bag open while tying the knots and then you will tie it closed when you are finished. After the first 9 knots, turn the bag right side and tie 9 more knots. Then turn the bag inside out again and tie 9 more knots. Repeat this until you have done it 9 times for a total of 81 knots. Then, add some graveyard dirt, salt, bluestone, lodestone, magnetic sand and a silver dime in the bag. Take the string with the 81 knots and wrap it around the bag and tie it closed. Carry it with you when playing games of chance.

Graveyard Love Work

Take a lock of hair from the man/woman who has strayed. Place this in a red bag. Bury the bag under the largest cross in the cemetery. Leave an offering of rum and bread on top of where you buried the bag. Leave the bag until the person returns to you. They won't be able to rest until they do. When your lover has returned, retrieve the bag and leave another offering of rum and bread. Keep the bag in a secret place.

To Make a Person Sick

Write the target's name on a piece of brown paper sack. Roll the paper up in black tar ball. Take the tar ball to the cemetery. Bury the tar ball with gunpowder, cayenne pepper and powdered wasp nest and the person will soon be ill.

Oya Offering for Business (Santeria)

Take a large fresh purple eggplant. Split it long ways but not all the way through. Place your business card inside. On top of the business card place a cup of brown sugar. Tie the eggplant together with 9 multi colored ribbons. Take the eggplant to the cemetery and place it along with a bottle of sangria at the front gate. Ask Oya to bring new business.

Stone Bowl

Take 9 stones from each of the following graves:

- Policeman for protection
- Wealthy person for money
- Doctor for health
- Hoodoo worker for magic
- Soldier for scouting out trouble
- Old person for wisdom
- Someone you loved for love and peace

Place the stones in a white bowl on your altar to bring these elements into your life.

To Bring Back a Person

Scrape a little dirt from the top of a woman's grave, over the heart area. Take it home and light 2 candles., one red and one black. Sprinkle the grave dirt in a circle around the candles. Take a piece of the target's clothes and lay them where they sleep. Open the Bible at random and read until the candles burn down. When the candles are burned all the way down, it is said the person will return.

To Keep the Law Away

To keep the law away, buy some graveyard dirt from a police officer. Make a purple doll baby and stuff it with the graveyard dirt. Take some red string and wrap it around the doll real tight, so as to bind the law. Keep the doll under your front porch.

Graveyard Rocks to Make Someone Move
Collect 9 rocks from a baby's grave. For nine nights in a row, take one of the rocks and toss it on the roof over the window of the person you want to move. As you toss the rock call out their name and tell them to move on.

To Make Someone Leave
This work is to make some leaves who lives in the same house as you. Go to the grave of a sinner 9 days after they have been buried. Dig elbow deep at the site of the left foot and grab some dirt. Be sure to get a good amount. Leave 15 cents in the hole and cover it up. Take the grave dirt and sprinkle it all around the outside of your home, going counterclockwise. Go inside and sprinkle some in the corners of your home. Take the remaining dirt and place it in a brown paper bag and throw it in a flowing river or other body of running water and it is said they will leave and never come back.

Bottle Spell to Haunt a Person
Go to the graveyard at midnight and bring a jar. Find an old unkempt grave and buy some graveyard dirt. Put the dirt in the jar along with something shiny and set the jar next to the grave. Tell the spirit it can go in the jar and play with the shiny object. Leave the jar there for 24 hours. Go back the next night at midnight and retrieve the jar. Leave 15 cents and a small bottle of rum at the gravesite. Close the jar. Then, take that jar to where your target lives and bury it under their front steps, porch, or somewhere in their front yard close to their front door. The closer you can get it to the door the better. Before you

cover it up, open the lid and remove the shiny object while telling the spirit what you want it to do. Then bury the jar. Using a metal piece of pipe, drive it down through the earth to the mouth of the bottle. Pull it back up, and you should have a plug of earth. Just toss that earth away and leave the hole. You have to be very discreet doing this so that the hole in the ground will not be noticed. It is said the spirit will escape from the bottle and enter the nearest abode, bothering the one who lives there until it is returned to its grave.

To Keep the Law Away

Buy some dirt from an infant's grave and mix it with sulfur and salt. Go around your home to each door and make a cross in front of the door on the ground with the mixture. As you make the cross, state your intention. This should be done in the mornings between eight and nine o'clock.

To Make Someone Return

This work is to make someone return who has run away for any reason. Go to a Catholic Graveyard and get a handful of dirt from a woman's grave from the chest area. Take that dirt and mix with 9 gourd seeds, 9 seeds from a red pepper and a sprinkling of sugar. Go to a crossroads and sprinkle some of the mixture there, right in the middle of the crossroads. Call out the person's name you want to return. Do this for three nights in a row and the one you want to come back will return.

To Get a Job Back

Well if you want a job of any kind, you get a dirt dauber and go to a baby's grave in the cemetery and reach your hand down in the same direction. And if you want a job anywhere, you mix the same dirt, the dirt dauber nest with the other dirt. And sprinkle it in front of the place and around the office where the boss has got to go in, and just say, "Little baby, in the name of the Father, Son and the Holy Ghost, give me my job back". And they give it to you. [Brunswick, Ga.] From "Hoodoo - Conjuration - Witchcraft - Rootwork" by Harry Middleton Hyatt

To Make a Wish Come True

Visit 3 cemeteries on a single night under the light of a full moon and gather dirt from the breast of nine graves of women and children and place in a red flannel bag. You should do this in complete silence for it to be effective. Concentrate on your desire intently as you do this. Leave a dime at each woman's grave and a little toy at each child's grave. Wear it on a string around your neck and next to your heart until your wish comes true.

To Make a Person Leave

To make a person leave, go to a graveyard at four o'clock in the morning and buy some dirt from a known philanderer. Mix the dirt with cayenne pepper and black salt and sprinkle it in the path of the person you want to leave and read Psalm 117. The person will soon be gone.

To Make a Person Pine Away

Make a doll baby to represent your target and stuff it with Spanish Moss. Put the doll in a miniature black coffin made out of pine. Write the person's name 9 times with red ink on the inside lid of the coffin. Cover the doll with dry pine needles before closing the lid. Take the little coffin to a cemetery and bury it. Stomp on the grave three times and say "I command you to disappear, just like that." Turn and leave, but not before paying the guardian of the cemetery 9 pennies at the gate.

To Bury a Bad Habit

For this work you will need to buy some dirt from the grave of a doctor. Make a black poppet and stuff it with the graveyard dirt, some yew, bay leaves and rosemary. Write down your bad habit on a piece of brown paper and place inside the doll baby and sew the doll closed. Take the doll to a cemetery and find a nice spot that has not been used as a grave yet. Bury the doll baby and your bad habit in the cemetery ground. Place some flowers on the grave and say your goodbyes to your habit. Leave a bottle of rum and fifteen cents at the cemetery gate for the guardian of the cemetery for allowing you to do your work there.

To Call a Spirit

Go to a cemetery at midnight and stand outside of the gate. Offer some coins and rum to the cemetery guardian. Make three calls with a ram's horn to the East, and call out "I wish to see (name)" three times. Grab a handful of dirt from where you stand and throw it towards the cemetery. Say, "Now, at the hour of midnight I want (name) to appear." If your request has been granted, the spirit will appear before dawn.

To Make a Person Move Home or Business

Go to a cemetery and gather a handful of grave dirt from seven different graves. Take the dirt home and dry it out if need be and grind it to a powder. Add some cayenne pepper, iron filings, and a dried toadstool that has been pulverized. Mix it up real good. Take some of that powder and throw it down at the front door of the person's home or place of business and it is said they will move shortly thereafter.

Cooking Supper for the Dead

Two people should cook it together, neither saying a word during the process. Get some dirt from the dead person's grave and set it in a saucer in the middle of the table. Cook something, such as turnip greens, that the dead person liked to eat, set the table for three and put up three chairs. Then bless the food without speaking to one another and start in silently to eat. Watch the third plate. Unseen hands will manipulate the knife and fork, greens will be taken from the dish all the time, but the chair will remain vacant. All will be well, but should you speak while your invisible guest is with you the wind will blow, the dogs bark, the chickens cackle, and thunder and lightning appear to frighten you (Puckett, 1926, pp. 102-103).

To Shame A Woman to Stop Running Around

Pound together a silver dime, some steel dust and graveyard dirt. Let the mixture sit for three days, then tie it up in a red flannel bag and carry it in your pocket. Put three small files under your "woman's" porch or walk—and then be absolutely unconcerned with her. Go out a lot at night—ignore her. No matter how much she has been running around she will be ashamed of herself and come back to you. Your charm has tied her to the house and gives her new interest in you (Puckett, 1926, p. 268).

To Kill Gossip

Get a beef tongue and cut a hole in it. Go to the cemetery at 6:00 in the evening on a new moon and buy some grave dirt from the grave of an evil person or from someone who was murdered. Dig down 2 inches at the breast and gather a lot of dirt. Leave $1.50 and a small bottle of rum as payment. Take some of that dirt and stuff it into the hole of that beef tongue. Slit the tongue down the middle and pour some more of that dirt in the middle and add Tabasco sauce and filé gumbo. Draw a rudimentary picture of the person or persons wagging their tongues using red ink if they are white and black ink of they are black. Write their names on the drawings 16 times each. Fold the paper up and tie it closed with white string if the person is white and black thread if the person is black. Stick them into the tongue and cover with cayenne pepper and the remaining grave dirt. Take nine new pins and stick them into the tongue, pinning both sides closed. Then wrap the tongue with a whole spool of thread—white for a white person and black for a black person, or both if both races.

Put the bound tongue in a brown paper bag and write "Rest in Peace" on the bag. Take the bag down to the cemetery and bury it at the foot of a big tree. As you do so, say "In the name of the Father, of the Son, and the Holy Ghost, shut your mouth!" The gossip should stop immediately.

For Good Luck

Go to the graveyard at midnight and buy some dirt from a gambling man's grave. Put it in your pocket with a High John the Conquer root and it is said your luck will instantly change for the better.

To Cause Confusion Between a Man and His Wife

Go to a cemetery and buy some dirt from the grave of a drunken gambler. Take the graveyard dirt and mix it with red pepper and black pepper and sprinkle it in the couple's house everywhere and it will cause confusion between the man and his wife.

For Protection Against Enemies

For protection from being crossed by an enemy, go to the grave of your nearest relative and buy some dirt from them. Dig a hole at the head of the grave and offer them one dollar. Take a tablespoon of dirt from the hole and stick that dollar bill into the hole and cover it up. Tell your relative you need their help to keep your enemies away from you. Take the dirt and sprinkle it in front of your home and you will be protected from then on.

To Cause Conflict

Graveyard dirt from a known gambler's grave is said to wreak havoc in the home when deployed with that intention. Go to a graveyard at midnight and buy some dirt from a notorious gambler's grave. Bring it home and spread it out to dry. Once it is dry, add a whole lot of red pepper and a ghost chili and mix it up real good. Be sure to wear gloves when making this powder. The next time you are in the home where you want to create conflict, sprinkle some of that graveyard dirt mixture around and it will cause the inhabitants of the home to fight for weeks on end.

Oya Blessing (Santeria)

Take a purple eggplant and a bottle of sangria and place it at the front gate or entrance to a cemetery. Ask Oya for her blessing.

Making the Four Corners

To have wishes granted quickly, you perform a rite called Making the Four Corners. For this work, you may choose to work in a smaller graveyard, though it is not necessary. Go to the graveyard where you do most of your work and enter the cemetery after knocking three times and asking permission. Leave 9 pennies at the gate. Go to each corner and kneel, making a wish and leaving fifteen cents. When you are finished with the fourth corner, go before St. Expedite either in a church or home altar and pray for quick results.

To Find a Lover

This work is for the person who is seeking a lover but has no one specific in mind. Before going to the cemetery, write down exactly the kind of person you want to spend your life with. Write down these qualities in red ink. Then write a definitive statement about having this ideal person in your life. Anoint the paper with Fire of Love Oil and fold the paper towards you three times. Take a red votive candle and anoint with Fire of Love Oil or Come to Me Oil and roll in magnetic sand. Take the candle and your petition paper to a graveyard and locate a mother's grave. If your own mother has passed and you are able to visit her grave, that is ideal. Set the candle on the grave in the heart area and bury the petition in the grave directly under the candle. Light the candle and say "In the name of the Father, the Son and the Holy Ghost, bring me my perfect lover." You should have a conversation with the spirit of the grave before doing this and let her know why you need her help. Leave some flowers and perfume and $1.50 as an offering for the spirit's help.

FORMULAS

Graveyard Fire Water

This is so much more than water. This mixture can be used to heat up any working. Take a clean glass jar to a cemetery when you know a storm is coming. Place the jar open in the back of the cemetery. When the storm has passed, retrieve the jar. Strain to remove debris. Add 21 of the hottest peppers you can get, 21 old pennies and 3 cups of white rum. Cap the jar and return to the cemetery. Bury the jar in the same spot you collected the water. Leave it for 21 days. When you retrieve the jar, leave offerings of flowers, tobacco and food. Use this mixture to heat up workings, cleanse away unwanted spirits and remove hexes.

Domination Oil

Use this oil for power over anyone or any situation.

- Lime
- Patchouli
- Vetivert
- Licorice Root
- Anise
- Pinch of graveyard dirt
- Pebble from a graveyard

Blend the above essential oils and roots in a base of mineral oil. Keep a piece of Licorice Root and a pebble from a graveyard in the master bottle.

Graveyard Power Dust

On a full moon gather dirt from under the first tree in 9 different cemeteries. Leave an offering of a silver dime under each tree. Mix all the dirts together along with dried basil, tobacco, nutmeg, dried rosemary, dried thyme, bay leaves, dried ginger, cinnamon and lavender powder. Grind everything into a fine powder and sift. Graveyard power dust adds power to mojo bags, gris gris and most workings.

Cemetery Oil

Place Graveyard Power Dust into a base oil. Allow to steep for 9 days. Strain and place in a clean glass jar. Add 3 drops of benzoin and keep in a cool dry place.

Get Away Powder

Mix up the following ingredients and toss it under the target's front steps or on their sidewalk where they will walk over it.

- Grave dirt
- Dirt from underneath your target's porch or from their front yard
- Cayenne pepper
- Dirt dauber nests
- Filet (powdered sassafras)
- Coffee grounds

Confusion Powder

Mix powdered grave dirt with powdered bluestone and sprinkle it where your enemy will be to cause them confusion.

Death Water

Take a bottle of cheap rum to the grave of a murderer. Open the bottle and pour half the bottle in an X on the grave. Place the half empty bottle in the area of the grave where the left hand would be. Tell the murderer you want death water. Stand with the bottle for one hour. Return home with the half empty bottle of rum. Add the following: goofer dust, datura seeds, snake skin, sulfur, coffin nails, asafetida, blood root, wormwood, and balmony. Cap the bottle and put in a dark place for 21 days. Splash this water anywhere an enemy will step in it.

Cemetery Nails

To make cemetery nails, wrap ordinary nails in burlap and bury at the cemetery entrance with offerings to the Guardian of the Cemetery. This can be 9 pennies and a small bottle of rum or whiskey, or an eggplant if offering to Oya. Leave them buried for a full month before retrieving them to allow time for them to rust. You can moisten the burlap if you want to speed up the process. Cemetery nails can be used as a substitute for coffin nails if you are unable to find real coffin nails. You can drive them into the ground at your adversary's home, throw them under your enemy's car, and toss around their home among other things.

Coffin Nail Oil

Add a coffin nail to a bottle of mineral oil with a pinch of graveyard dirt and a piece of a human finger bone for a potent crossing oil.

LAGNIAPPE: GOOFER DUST

Lagniappe (pronounced *lan-yapp*) is a gesture of southern hospitality where you throw in a little something extra at the point of sale to show sincere appreciation. The meaning of the word has expanded over time to be applicable to any situation where you offer a little something extra in a given situation. We offer you this brief section on goofer dust as a little lagniappe for our readers.

What is Goofer Dust?

Goofer dust? Well, goofer dust is just - it just a kind that people use. At any time you use anything from hoodoo - some call it hoodoo, some call it goofer. But any time that you use a dust that you use to sprinkle - like if you come to me and say, "I'm upsetted in my home it seems like things ain't going right. I want you to give me something to sprinkle my home with, see if I can bring peace. "Well, I'll give you some thing that you go into your house. I give you anything to scrub, that would cause peaceful power. Well, you just take that and sprinkle it round. People call that goofer dust. Well, that just the common term they got - the term that is ordinary used in hoodoo. [New Orleans, La., (828), 1218: 1.]

Goofer Dust Formulas

There is no standard formula for goofer dust. Each rootworker has their own formula, though there are some commonalities amongst formulas. A couple of ingredients you will find in most goofer dust formulas is graveyard dirt, powdered snake skin and some kind of insect or bone.

Formula 1
Mix the following ingredients for a powerful goofer dust:

- Dirt from the grave of 9 criminals
- Gunpowder
- Black pepper
- Red pepper
- Powdered feathers from a black rooster
- Powdered snake skin
- Sulfur
- Powdered human bone

Formula 2
- Dirt from a sinner's grave
- Powdered poisonous insects
- Powdered rattlesnake sheds
- Cayenne pepper

Formula 3
- Powdered scorpion
- Powdered spider
- Powdered mud dauber nest
- Graveyard dirt

Goofer Dust Work

Goofer dust is mostly used in foot track magic, just like hot foot powder. Following are a couple of ways to use goofer dust that are a departure from the usual throwing it down in the path of a target.

Revenge On An Enemy

Take a fresh brown egg and make a small hole in both ends. Carefully blow out the inside of the egg. Carefully and with patience fill the egg with goofer dust. At 3 am, throw the egg against the home or business door of the enemy.

To Get a Job

Make a goofer dust out of powdered snake sheds, patchouli leaf and magnetic sand. Rub your hands with it and rub it all over your body and behind your ears before going to a job interview and it is said you will get the job.

To Make a Person Have Sore Feet

Make up some goofer dust from cayenne pepper, dirt dauber nest and grave dirt. Dust the inside of your target's shoes with it and it is said they will have sore feet that are slow to heal.

REFERENCES

Billops, C., Dodson, O. and Van Der Zee, J. (1978). *The Harlem Book of the Dead*. New York: Morgan and Morgan.

Cemetery Research and Gravestone Rubbings.....a How To, site. (n.d.). Retrieved from http://www.angelfire.com/ut/gmachoocho/cemetery411.html

Graham, J. S. (n.d.) "FOLK MEDICINE," *Handbook of Texas Online* (http://www.tshaonline.org/handbook/online/articles/sdf01), accessed August 07, 2012. Published by the Texas State Historical Association.

The Graven Images of Bethel Cemetery - Croton Friends of History. (n.d.). Retrieved from http://www.crotonfriendsofhistory.org/bethel-cemetery/

Headstone Icons, Symbols and Their Meanings: ANIMALS. (n.d.). Retrieved from http://www.iacpinc.org/cemeteryicons.pdf

Hyatt, H. M. (1970). *Hoodoo-Conjuration-Witchcraft-Rootwork Vol. 1-5*. Hannibal, MO: Alma Egan Hyatt Foundation.

McMickle, N. A. (2002). *An Encyclopedia of African American Christian Heritage*, Judson Press.

North by South, (n. d.). *Conch Shells - North by South/ Great Migrations Page.* (n.d.). Retrieved from http://northbysouth.kenyon.edu/1998/death/conchshells.htm

Pinn, A., Finley, S. C., and Alexander, T. (2009) *African American religious cultures, Volume 1,* ABC-CLIO.

Puckle, B.S. (1926). *Funeral Customs: Their Origin and Development.* Retrieved from http://www.sacred-texts.com/etc/fcod/fcod11.htm

Puckett, N. (1926). *Folk beliefs of the southern Negro.* University of North Carolina Press.

TheCemeteryClub. (n.d.). *Symbols.* Retrieved from http://www.thecemeteryclub.com/symbols.html

Wakden, B. B. (1976). *To Rub or Not to Rub,* Woodstock, New York: Lithe-Art Press.

Walker, J. G. (1972). *Stranger Stop and Cast an Eye: A Guide to Gravestones and Gravestone Rubbing.* Brattleboro, Vermont: The Stephen Greene Press,

Wright, R and Hughes, W. III. (1996). *Lay Down Body: Living History in African American Cemeteries.* New York: Visible Ink Press.

RESOURCES

1) Planet Voodoo—For authentic New Orleans Voodoo, hoodoo, conjure and rootwork supplies and services: altar dolls, conjure oils, herbs and roots, gris gris, curios, floor washes, spiritual waters, incense, jewelry, ju ju, sachet powders, spirit bottles, voodoo dolls, wanga dolls and pakets, doll babies, and zombies. www.planetvoodoo.com

2) Root Mama Conjure—Offering the finest in authentic occult items all handcrafted within the boundaries of sacred ritual for the modern world. All items are dedicated to bringing unique and powerful tools for the experienced and beginning practitioner. In true Hoodoo fashion, most items by are crafted using found, natural and recycled items making them unique and one of a kind. www.rootmamaconjure.com

3) Crossroads Mojo—For all things related to crossroads conjure and more! Poppets and doll babies, conjure oils, jewelry and fetishes. www.crossroadsmojo.com

4) Medicines and Curios—complete inventory of spiritual supplies, old-fashioned natural remedies, curios, botanicals, magickal oils, herbs, candles, sachet powders, spiritual baths and more! www.medicinesandcurios.com

5) Crossroads University—Learn traditional, southern style conjure and rootwork. The mission of Crossroads University is to preserve the integrity of traditional indigenous magical and spiritual technologies and healing systems and conserve the diverse cultural heritage of the American South. Open enrollment. www.crossroadsuniversity.com

6) Planet Voodoo's Conjure Corner—The forum and virtual campus for Crossroads University. Learn all about New Orleans Voodoo and Hoodoo and southern conjure. One need not be a student to join. Warm, friendly and nonjudgmental atmosphere! www.conjurecorner.com

7) Creole Moon's Conjure Club—Get monthly ebooks such as this one in digital form each month plus weekly downloads for one low fee of $6.00 per month. www.creolemoon.com

About the Authors

Denise Alvarado is a native Creole born and raised in the Voodoo and hoodoo rich culture of New Orleans, Louisiana. She is an artist and independent researcher with advanced degrees in cultural anthropology and psychology. She is the author of several books, including the *Voodoo Hoodoo Spellbook* and the *Hoodoo Almanac 2012*, coauthored with Carolina Dean and Alyne Pustanio. She is also the founder and Editor in Chief of Hoodoo and Conjure Magazine. Denise is a medicine woman and rootworker in the southern Hoodoo tradition with over 40 years of life experience in the conjure arts and mysticism.

Madrina Angelique was born and raised in rural Georgia. She has immersed herself in the study and practice of traditional southern hoodoo since childhood. She is initiated in the Palo tradition as Madre Nganga of Munanso Centella Ndoki Nkuyo Malongo Corta Lima Cordosa, initiated by Chief Ololele Afolabi, godson of Tata Antonio Ali. She is also initiated in Santeria as Iyalorisha of Ile Ori Yemaya, initiated by Baba Ogun Solu, godson of Chief Bolu Fantunmise of the Ifa Orisha Cultural Center in Nigeria and Atlanta. Madrina is a regular contributor to Hoodoo and Conjure Magazine and coauthor of *13 Legendary Crossroads Rituals* with Denise Alvarado.

TO OUR READERS

Creole Moon Publications is a small independent publisher specializing in the cultural and spiritual traditions and folklore of the American South. Our mission is to publish quality books that observe and preserve the southern cultural heritage and folk magic traditions that enrich people's lives.

Our readers are our most important resource, and we appreciate your input, suggestions, and ideas about what you would like to see published.

Visit our website at *www.creolemoon.com* to learn about our upcoming books and downloads, and to sign up for our Conjure Club, newsletters and exclusive offers.

You can also contact us at creolemoon@planetvoodoo.com or at

Creole Moon Publications
P.O. Box 25687
Prescott Valley, AZ. 86312

Printed in Great Britain
by Amazon.co.uk, Ltd.,
Marston Gate.